WE, THE WOMEN

*For Annette
a good neighbor
and friend

from
Elaine*

WE, THE WOMEN

Limericks Liberated

by

Elaine Watson

RENO PRESS / DEARBORN, MICHIGAN

*To Bill, whose books of limericks—
for men—inspired me to write a few
limericks for women*

Copyright © 1980
by Elaine Watson

All rights reserved.

No material in this book may be copied,
reproduced, or used in any way
without written permission.

Library of Congress Catalog Card No. 80-51132

Send orders to:

RENO PRESS
16 Adams Lane
Dearborn, Michigan 48120

Manufactured in the United States of America by
Harlo Press, 50 Victor, Detroit, Michigan 48203

INTRODUCTION

Most modern American limericks are written for men—about eager nymphomaniacs. Or about young ladies who for some unaccountable reason like to ride tigers.

WE, THE WOMEN explores in limerick form a good many of the hangups American women have about themselves, about men, and about the culture they grew out of.

The classic limerick contains a lot of folk wisdom. In a hundred years, should people want to understand lifestyles of their ancestors, they might well look at some of our humorous light verse. If we can keep a sense of humor about our problems, so pundits say, the chances are we will keep our sanity, too.

WE, THE WOMEN touches on a good many subjects.

Modern technology, for example, scares a few women, but it fascinates others. Changes in familiar family relationships turn the world upside down for some women. Others like change. Some women deplore macho males, some find them amusing, and others use them.

Women often look at the lives of people who lived in the past with envy, or laughter, or horror, but the blunt satire of a limerick can put romantic ideas about history into perspective.

Read WE, THE WOMEN for fun. For a belly laugh now and then. But while you read you will be sharing the lives of modern American females. Of Marilyn the typist, who wanted to be a musician. Of terrible driver Maybelle, whose children had long left the nest. Of tiny Ann and fat Lenore. Of Suzanne, who sang to her plants. Of the young woman who was swamped by statistics. And of many, many more.

A lot of the limericks in this book have a sassy line at the end. Some finish with an ironic twist.

In every one the reader will recognize an acquaintance or a part of herself—or of himself.

CONTENTS

PART ONE
OF WOMEN AND MEN 9

PART TWO
MOTHERING 21

PART THREE
WOMEN IN HISTORY AND FANTASY 29

PART FOUR
OTHER WOMEN ARE A LOT OF FUN 41

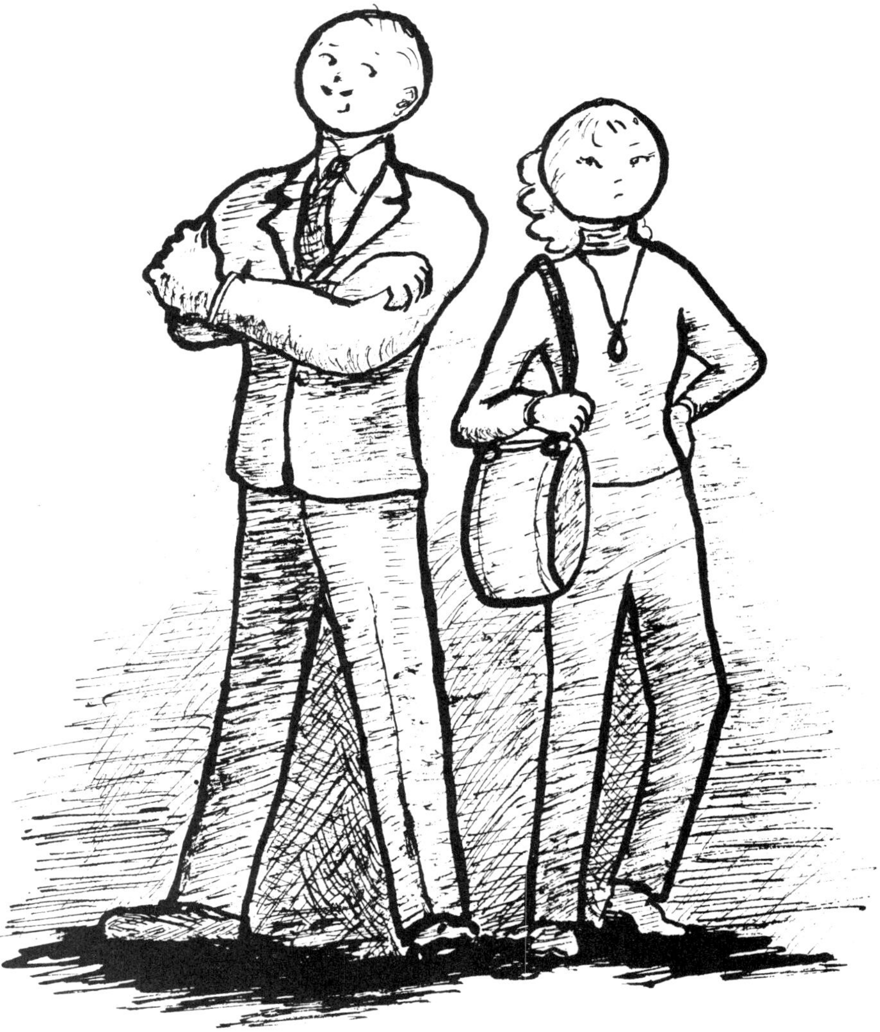

PART ONE

OF WOMEN AND MEN

"It's my manhood she envied," he thought,
"Or my muscles or mustache she sought."
   But the envy *she* bore
   Was for riches galore
His executive's salary bought.

"It's that extra, but weak, chromosome,"
Said Professor J. Macho Jerome,
    "That makes woman miss out on
    The fun man can count on—
And even a sexy, bald dome."

There once was a siren named Jill
Who dispensed all her favors at will.
    Her teasing attracted
    And kept men distracted
So they toiled without reaching the till.

There was a young doctor from Dexter
Whose husband rebelled and it vexed her.
    He would not do the dishes
    Nor accede to her wishes.
His reluctance completely unsexed her.

There was a smart girl at Depauw
Who doted on George Bernard Shaw.
    When a male asked, "Cohabit?"
    She said, quick like a rabbit,
"If I'm well-protected by law!"

Jane's boyfriend thought it was a joke
When she puffed a cigar with her coke.
    Jane's taste vexed her lover.
    She said, "You'll recover,
But a good cigar is a smoke!"

"When I man-watch," says Melanie Means,
At the bar rail where she sometimes leans,
    "It's very distracting.
    I often find lacking
The requirements to fill out their jeans."

A man calls a girl who is pretty
His sweet little amorous kitty.
   But when kit becomes cat
    That man might say "Scat!"
If he's macho—or even a Mitty.

At the rest home spry Mrs. McFall
Said, "Parties have not changed at all.
   When young, boys were shy,
   And now, old men die,
And leave us alone at the ball!"

If the artist were *Mm.* Manet
Would those bathers so tres toujour gai[1]
   Cavort a la nu[2]
   And try faire la roue?[3]
No, the *men* would shed duds. Enchanté!

1 — *happy*
2 — *in the nude*
3 — *to show off*

Her honey's hung up on the Stones.
His image of females is clones
    Of wild, willing women
    With no future in 'em
But for their erogenous zones.

A woman named Simone Legree
Kept her office staff tuned—to a T.
    Said they one to another,
    "Give me back to Big Brother!
'Cause she's just like a mother to me!"

There was a tail-gater named Mary
Who said she would no longer tarry
    To watch *that* stupid game.
    The men said, "It's a shame.
But your duties are done. So long, Mary!"

There was a young wife full of graces
Whose husband bought delicate laces
   And her baby-doll clothes.
Then she cried, "Dear, I froze!
Warmer women give warmer embraces!"

For most of the girls in O'Sage
Virginity's now all the rage.
    No hustlers nor groupies
    Nor "uncles" with toupees
Can trade in room keys in O'Sage!

"I want you to meet," said Pol Pearl,
"My lover, named Samuel Searle.
    Since so long we have tarried
    Without getting married
I'm called Pearl-Searle and Sammy's
    Searle-Pearl."

When Jenny was five she got trains.
And when she was eight it was planes.
    Jenny's turning thirteen
    Made it clear to be seen
Planning "unisex" bends only brains!

A sexist astronomer, Janet,
Saw only one feminine planet.
   Said she, "If I find
   An orb of that kind
And they use a *god's* name, I will ban it!"

A fat fraulein chortled, "Mein Herr,
I give you a frohliche dare:
   I will drink more Beir than you
   Till the gastgebers ban you
And, betrunken, you fall off your chair!"

"Young ladies are not too refined,"
Said Abner Peabody. "I find
   I can't tell the girls
   From the boys. Said the girls,
"What *does* the old fool have in mind?"

There once was a woman of thirty
Who was known to be friendly and flirty.
    When asked if she'd wed
    She'd say, "Ask me instead
How I'd choose, when *all* men are so purty!"

When a young wife who lived in North Bay
Was showered with flowers she'd say,
    "Though your loving, my dear,
    Always fills me with cheer,
I'd prefer just a daisy a day."

A young woman who lived in St. Paul
Stood in stockings just seven feet tall.
   When asked whom she'd wed
     She grinned as she said,
"A man whose prospectus 'snot small!"

There was a quite sassy old crone
Who wed a curmudgeon named Stone.
   When asked why they'd wed
     She cackled and said,
"It's as close as we'd get to a clone."

The work of an angel was rough.
He had to be made of stern stuff.
   No soft human feeling
     Nor womanly wealing
Dared make him less righteous and tough!

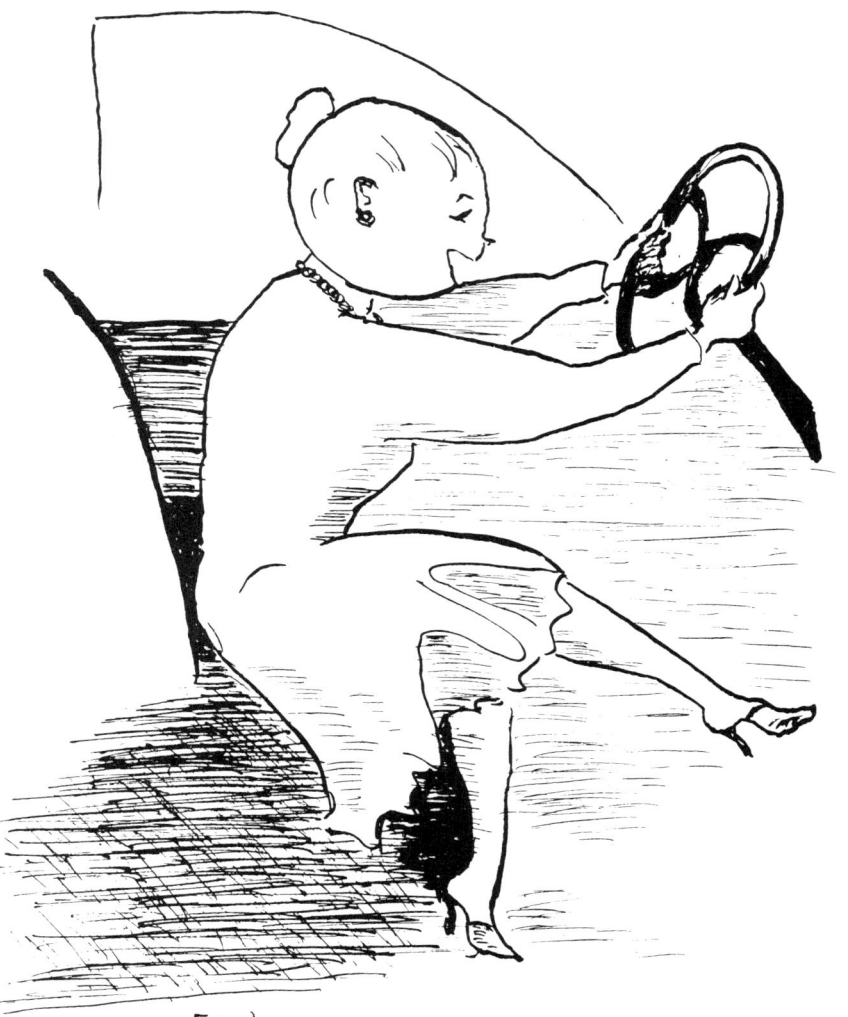

E.W.

PART TWO
MOTHERING

A matron named Maybelle Perone
While driving caused many a groan.
   She crept down the streets
     Yelling "Kids! Keep your seats!"
Forgetting she now drove alone.

The woman who lived in a shoe
Would have Freudians in a real stew.
   Was it brothel or home?
   Had her man left to roam?
Did her kids warp their ids with that shrew?

An immigrant mother from Split
Swore her child drove her into a fit.
   "It's your language!" she cried.
   "Cheer up, Mom," daughter sighed.
"I promise you! No more bullshit!"

"My sitter's a good one," said Joan,
"And at last by the sea I'm alone.
   So why do I screech
   And run from the beach
Every time that I hear the darn phone?"

A terrible cook was Ma Lorne.
Her chowder was far below norm.
   When her children rebelled
     And her gaunt husband yelled
She knew she'd cooked up a real storm!

A pilot named Fifi complained
(Though her skill in a plane was acclaimed)
   "If mother had known
   The way the wind's blown
She'd have left her poor daughter unnamed!"

A physicist long out of Yale
Meets symposiums—each without fail.
   Yale symposiums? Nay.
   'Tis the school P.T.A.
For her there'll be no cakes and ale.

The relatives gaily confide
Aunt Maudie turned tricks on the side.
   But if daughter makes eyes
   At the neighborhood guys
Her mother is fit to be tied!

A woman with two under three
Was asked if the Movement should be
    A mom's chief avocation.
    Sighed she, with aspiration,
"One a day is sure plenty for me!"

There was a wan Mom from Peoria
Who had a teenager named Gloria.
    Mom cried, "I'll behead
    That crackpot who said,
'Raising youngsters will tend to restore ya'!"

A grandma named Jane came from Maine.
She was always off flying her plane.
    When asked to play sitter
    She'd say, "But I'm fitter
To fly than to sit." Right on, Jane!

A Skinner-box baby had tried
Once she'd grown, to be happy outside.
    "It's a brave world," she said.
    "But there's too much I dread.
It was better with no place to hide!"

Her daughter's out camping with Joe.
She says it's the best way to go.
   Her mom says to her, "Chum,
   Selling cheap's pretty dumb!
Tell that cheap camper Joe to go blow!"

"I can't please my mom," said Trish Jones.
"We talk 'mid her moans and my groans.
   She tries to think young
   But her lifestyle is hung
On those middle-aged shackles and bones!"

Senora Carmel was quite old.
Did her child turn her out in a cold
   Nursing home to be cared for?
   Of course not! She'd prepared for
All relations her casa could hold!

E.W.

PART THREE

WOMEN IN HISTORY AND FANTASY

In this section a word or two of explanation might be helpful.

Some of the women in History and Fantasy were not Americans, but they are a part of our heritage.

If the Venus de Milo had arms
And she held an old hoe from the farms
    Or a cookbook, perhaps,
    Or a chamber pot, chaps,
Would she still fill the bill with her charms?

This Elizabeth sure was no saint
And her Mary showed little restraint.
   But both wrote up a storm,
   Keeping gossips' tongues warm
And making faint-hearted types faint.

Elizabeth Wollstonecraft, who was a lively English feminist in the late eighteenth century, wrote "Vindication of the Rights of Women."

Both her writing and her lifestyle caused quite a stir.

She died in childbirth.

Her daughter Mary wrote the novel FRANKENSTEIN.

At seventeen Mary eloped with the poet Percy Bysshe Shelley, while his first wife Harriet was still living.

But Harriet soon killed herself, and then Mary became Mary Shelley.

Scandal, scandal.

A woman named Dolley cried, "Run!
Those Limeys are having their fun!
   Though my week's washing burns
   [As every child learns]
I must try to save Washington!"

Dolley Madison, so they say, hung her washing in the East Room of the White House.
But she had her priorities in order.
In 1814, when the British burned the city of Washington, Dolley ran back to rescue the Gilbert Stuart portrait of Geo. W. in the White House, and thus she saved it for posterity.
So they say.

"Bring my hat and my hatchet to me,"
Cried prayerful, gigantic Carrie.
   "That saloon first we'll tackle
   Then we'll break every shackle
On those voting booths! Yea, verily!"

Carrie Nation was a giant of a woman—in many ways. Not awfully popular in her own time, but then reformers of either sex do cause problems.
Even today.

When asked how Ben Franklin performed
Old Mistress McKay raged and stormed,
   "That puppy was hateful!
   He said I should be grateful.
I'd just wanted my cold bedsheets warmed."

Remember Benjamin Franklin's eighth reason in his "Reasons For Preferring An Elderly Mistress" (1748)?
*   "Make use of older women," he wrote. "They're so grateful."*

Poor Eve never had any fun.
Twixt a rib and an apple she won
   A bad reputation
   For male mutilation
And tempting fruit good guys should shun.

*   Eve was formed from Adam's rib.*
*   Because of her, so they say, Adam lost a rib and the Garden of Eden, too.*

Jane Austen smiled, sipping her nectar
And reading sage hints from earth's sector
   For mothers and daughters.
   Their wisdom oft caught hers,
But Jane's genius made more folks respect her.

Long after current, more strident commentaries on mother-daughter relationships have been forgotten, readers will still love Jane Austen!

Cinderella soon learned being poor
With big feet might have had its allure.
   She cried, at the palace,
   "Oh, Godmother, alas!
I've discovered the prince is a boor!"

Foot fetish is hardly new.
Poor Cinderella.
At least she had the royal jewels.

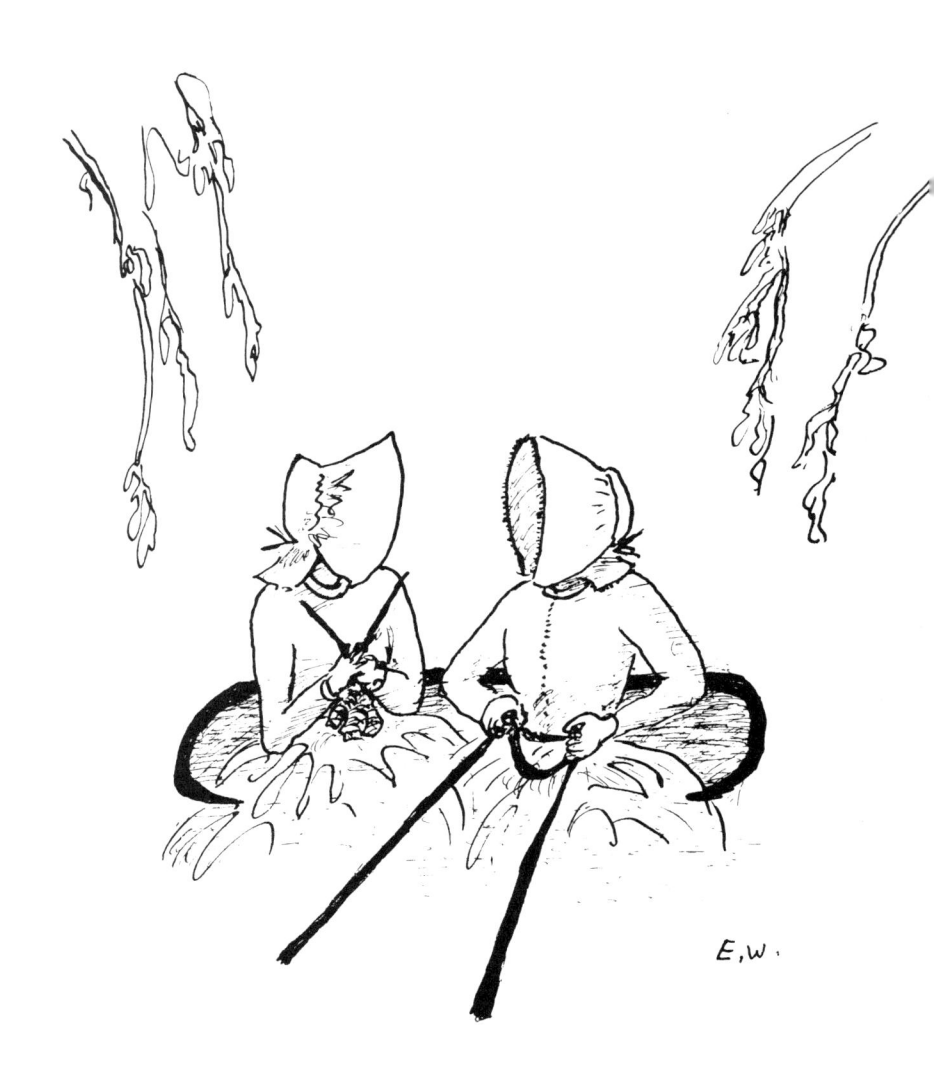

E.W.

When the telephone wasn't invented
How were feminine woes represented?
   With families big
   Or with travel by gig
Women talked out their cares unresented.

   A "gig" was a light horsedrawn vehicle with two wheels. Great for leisurely chatting, hour after hour.
  But with no air conditioning.
  We win a little and lose a little.

"If you take our boy, watch for attack,"
Sobbed Sarah to Abe. "With no knack
　　For eluding the murders
　　Done by robbers or herders
He could die with a knife in his back!"

After all the agony Sarah—who was barren until she was ninety—must have suffered while she carried and gave birth to Isaac, apparently her husband Abraham failed to consult her when he took the boy off to murder (excuse, please, sacrifice) him.
　　However, all went well, as you may recall. If you don't, read it in GENESIS sometime.
　　It's a harrowing story.

　．"Those poor Western women," sighed Chiu
As she ate a fat egg roll or two,
　　"With their big feet unbound
　　They all teeter around
Doing men's work and women's work, too!"

The custom in old China of binding girl babies' feet was cruel.
　　But the pampered adult that resulted might have looked out of her "cage" at frantic, driven women in the West, and smiled.

Poor frantic Calpurnia from Roma
Cried, "Don't leave, Dear! I'll sink into a coma!
   I've just had a bad dream.
   Things are not what they seem.
In Rome there's a rotten aroma!"

   Shakespeare created for Julius Caesar's wife Calpurnia a nightmare that foretold bad news for her husband on the Ides of March.
   Otherwise would anyone remember Caesar's wife's name?

Folks called Mary Lincoln a shrew
For she bullied the whole White House crew.
   Said she, "*I* give you *my* pledge,
   If he'd married Ann Rutledge,
You'd have mean Mrs. *Douglas* to rue!"

   This is a myth every school child used to encounter.
   Maybe Lincoln had a thing for Ann Rutledge. Maybe not.
   But Mary Lincoln did get to be a shrew while trying to teach Abe some social amenities.

Since that wolf ate Red Riding Hood's granny
Sexists search into each nook and cranny
   For meaning. But then
   He was just *hungry* when
He jumped into bed with old granny.

One wearies of analysis and analysis and analysis, mostly Freudian.
   Hunger is a basic drive, too.

Could a flag-making seamstress named Ross
Have earned fame as a Federal boss?
   Good George praised her instead
   With a pat on the head,
Defining her role—and his loss.

Maybe Betsy Ross was not an intellectual, or even strong on charisma.
   But then maybe she was.
   Who will ever know?

"Grow old, Dear, alongside of me,"
Said Rob to Elizabeth B.
   But twixt babies and bouts with her lover
   Her genius could scarcely recover.
Ba died young. Rob lived—heartily.

Elizabeth Barrett, as you may recall, was a sickly woman who found happiness when she left her possessive father to marry fellow-poet Robert Browning. (Her family called her "Ba.")

During her short happiness (and pregnancies and general decline in health) she wrote a little lovely poetry.

Robert wrote a lot of poems, and one of them that he addressed to her began, "Grow old along with me!/The best is yet to be,/The last of life for which the first was made."

Robert Browning lived a long, long time.

Cleopatra won everyone's heart
Only partly because she was smart.
   If you've got a big river
   And a crown to deliver
You're a few jumps ahead at the start.

Cleopatra's river, of course, was the Nile.
Her crown represented the throne of Egypt.
And the hearts? The hearts of Julius Caesar and Mark Antony, among others.

E.W.

PART FOUR

OTHER WOMEN ARE A LOT OF FUN

There was a young woman named Ms. Sticks
Who tried to conform to statistics.
   She kept track of her calories,
   Her TV's, and her salaries,
Her orgasms, and other logistics.

Her training for flying was rough.
Competition was equally tough.
    But when her time came
    For national fame
Her attraction was called "Powder Puff."

Beneath her size 38D
Beat a heart that was open and free.
    But the peek-a-boo blouse
    And hot tub in the house
Came along when she'd turned fifty-three!

There was a fine female named Caucus
Whose laughter was hearty and raucous.
    She'd tell "masculine" jokes
    With the best of the blokes,
Which startled the timid and vacuous.

"Why is it," sighed farmer Grace Shield,
"If my livelihood comes from the field
   I'm not 'chic' at the Fair
   Like the ladies who share
Little jellies their small gardens yield?"

There was a young actress named Mars
Who smoked long, black Cuban cigars.
   When asked if she should—
   If a chic woman would—
She said, "Red black cigars suit us stars!"

A clean-living hitcher named Lotta
Rode easy from Maine to Yawata.
   But when she got back
   They found pot in her pack.
She at once was persona non grata.

When asked how she'd managed to reach
Ninety, Audrey had little to teach.
    "Did you keep a strict diet?"
    "Lordy, no! But I'll try it
When I'm back from my bash at the beach!"

There was a contralto named Tess
Whose avoirdupois was a mess.
    Since she's fifty pounds slighter
    (Though vibrato's much lighter)
Her claque performs with no duress.

There was a young geisha named Lotus
With a doctorate out of Duns Scotus.
    When asked if she cared
    How her talents were shared,
She said, "Mere operandi modus!"

A woman named Gertrude MacPhee
Was chairman of each committee
   That most anyone formed.
   Every chair that she warmed
Exuded her hot energy.

Annette adored Proust and Monet
While Sal watched sit-com's every day.
   She'd dropped out of school.
   People called her a fool.
So "chacun son gout!"* Who's to say?

*"chacun son gout": everyone to his own taste

There was a young woman named Joy
Whose portrait indeed seemed to cloy.
   "It's a pity," she sighed.
   "I'm sorry I tried
To buy brushwork by boys from PLAYBOY."

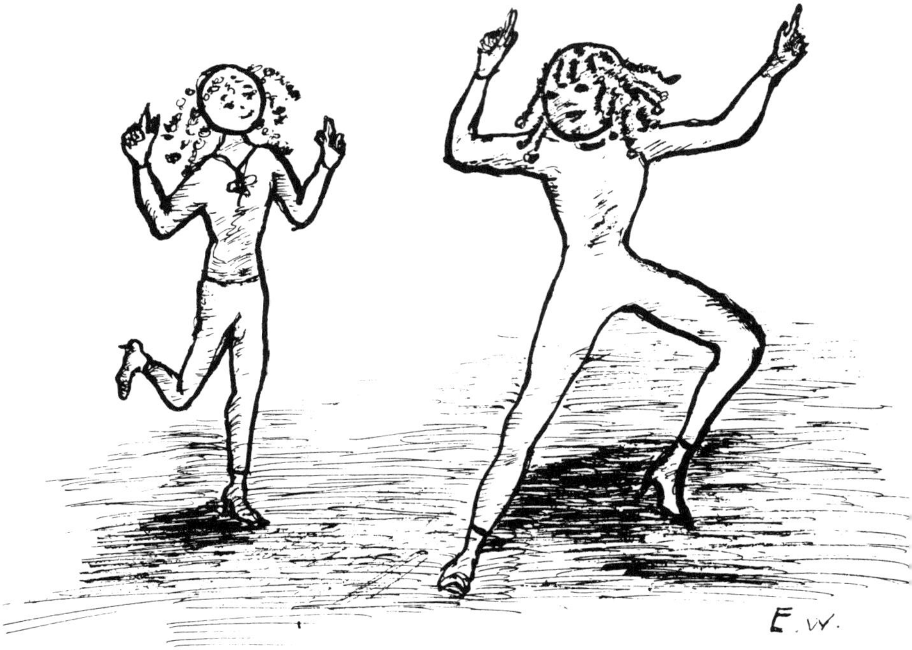
E.W.

A woman whose name is Lanette
Knows her cadences will never get
    Through to friends whose white skin
    Keeps their libidos in.
Lanette kindly indulges them, yet.

There was a young genius named Marilyn
Who yearned to perform on the violin.
    But her long fingers tease
    Just the typewriter keys
While her heart sings along with the carrilon.

A guru named Mr. Molloy
Tells women the *smart* hoi-polloi
    Wearing stockings and skirts
    Among trousers and shirts
Will turn dollars and cents into joy.

A woman named Agnes McGee
Decided to learn how to ski.
    While attempting to schuss
    Her pole smacked her puss
And she schussed *round* the hill, recklessly.

Her red nose roused laughter in some
And others declared she was dumb.
    But they kept their thoughts inward
    Eating grapes from her vineyard
Because she had such a green thumb.

A middle-aged woman named Pearl
Gave the pumpkin seed* habit a whirl.
    Then she swore off the pills
    As a cure for her ills
And turned into a hot-tempered churl.

*(term commonly used for hormone pills)

A woman named Eleanor Hoppe
Vowed the thrill of her life was to shop.
   "My dreams there," she said,
   "Are not just in my head.
When I drop in to shop I can't stop!"

A fiddler called Katie O'Flynn
Changed her name into Kathleen O. Lynn.
   She pulled her hair back
   And changed her attack
And captured first chair violin.

There was a fat girl named Lenore
Who measured her girth by the score.
   When a willowy model
   Looked askance at her waddle
She floored the discourteous bore.

A plumber named Ada had class.
At the airport she cried out "Alas!"
   (She'd been plunged into tourist
   With credentials the purist)
"I've never known plunging so crass!"

There once was a countess named Clare
Whose decollete dipped down to *there*.
   When questioned, she sighed,
   "I've got nothing to hide,
And a lot that I'm willing to share!"

There was a chic matron named Lou
With a registered show dog named Pooh.
   Though Pooh was a winner
   He'd never take dinner
Near his owner, like mongrel dogs do.

There was a young sexpot, Ms. Cleon
Whose hair lighted up just like neon.
   When asked if she wore it
   So men would adore it
She said, "Darling, it's just to turn *me* on!"

Melinda could have worn size 8
While Katherine was called Two-ton Kate.
   Lin's outfits were baggy
   With shoes big and craggy.
But Kate showed each ounce of her weight.

There was a great linguist who'd boast
She could order food better than most.
   But a roach made her scared
   And she softly said, "Merde!"
She was served lumpy gravy on toast.

Yevette leaves her cake 'till it burns.
She'll rescue the mess when she learns—
   With a mark in her book
   And her phone off the hook—
What happens on "As The World Turns."

E.W.

"When I bowl, my small problem astounds,"
Sighed Ann, who weighed eighty-eight pounds.
   "If I throw lane or gutter
    My whole team starts to sputter
For I follow the ball where it bounds!"

There was a pot-maker named Dot.
Throwing pots always cheered her a lot.
   Said she, "Guess I'll steal
   An hour at my wheel.
When my pots send me, I don't need pot!"

Women often have cause to rebel
While they torture their bodies like hell
   To fit masculine strictures
   They'd made happier pictures
With designers like Coco Chanel.

A woman named Sarah Price-Jones
Said, "My peer group is filled with great moans.
   Though my background is WASP
    My hands like to grasp
Greasy wrenches instead of sleek roans."

A little old woman, a witch,
Sold her friends many black charms to pitch
   Lots of enemies cell-ward,
   And even some hell-ward.
Pushing evil eyes made this witch rich.

Melinda went searching for roots.
She wore clothes from Cardin and Blass boots.
   In Nairobi she heard
    A loud whispered word:
"A whitey! That kind burns and loots!"

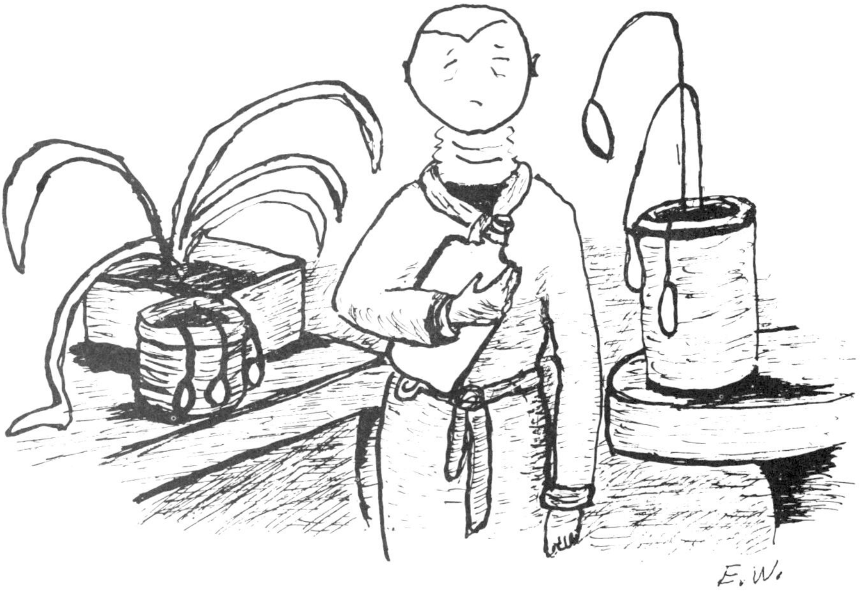
E.W.

When Suzanne had a house filled with plants
Their culture she'd greatly enhance.
   She sang to them nightly,
   Which kept them all sprightly.
Laryngitis, though, sank Suzanne's plants.

"Dear Abby," neurotic Nan penned,
"Your selected anthologies send
  Me running for cover
  When I start to discover
The hangups you think you can mend."

There was a young biker who'd parley
With others whose tempers were knarley.
  "I'm not macho," she said,
  "But like them I see red
When cars try to sideswipe my Harley!"

Her Weight-Watcher's diet she found
Was dismal in spite of the sound
   Of the glamorous ads
   From dollar-wise lads
Who gained whene'er she lost a pound.

There was a young housewife from Dayton
Whose doctor kept patients all waitin'.
   After three hours lost
   Her appointment she tossed.
With Krishna she's now meditatin'.

At last she became Ph.D.
Her mind soared with brilliance to be.
   With her doctorate's claim
   She still signs her name
For her food stamps. She signs brilliantly.

When polled, Sally said, "I declare
I've ideas I'm willing to share.
   But their questions were framed
   To get answers they claimed
To be true. They've caught *me* in their snare!"

Though Molly Malone loved to dance
The dance floor she'd hardly enhance.
   When she tripped the fantastic
   All her movements were spastic
And she burst through the seams of her pants.

This economist always abjures
Relying on feminine lures.
   If her colleagues can't cope
   And she wants the straight dope
She just consults Standard and Poor's.

A woman of years named Ms. Gale
Found her tired heart had started to fail.
   "I'll get a bypass,"
    Said the plucky old lass.
"I want one more degree out of Yale!"

Elaine Watson's verse has appeared in the *Christian Science Monitor*, *The Lyric*, *Poetry View*, *The Poet*, and *Peninsula Poets*, among other publications, and in two anthologies, *Forty Salutes to Michigan Poets* and *Echoes From the Moon*. She teaches English at Henry Ford Community College in Dearborn, Michigan, and belongs to the Michigan Poetry Society and the Detroit Women Writers.